CONTENTS

FRANCE IN THE EARLY NINETEENTH CENTURY

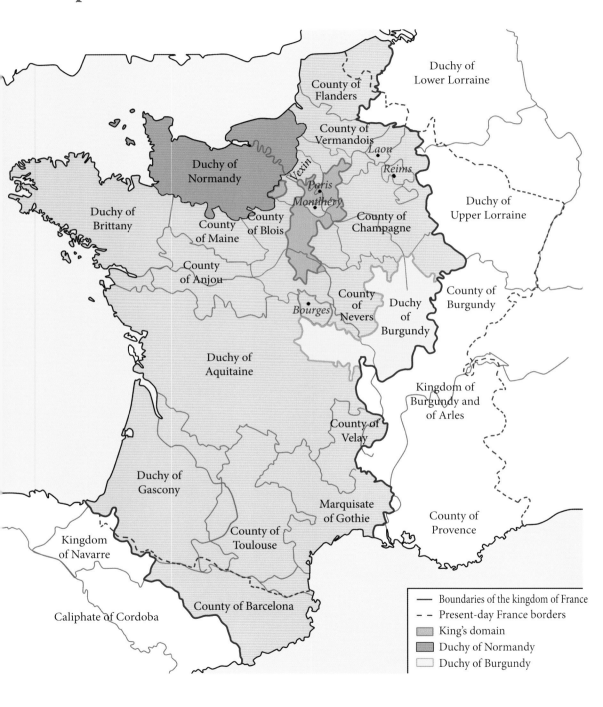

County of Flanders

Duchy of Lower Lorraine

County of Vermandois

Laon

Reims

Duchy of Normandy

Vexin

Paris

Montlhéry

Duchy of Upper Lorraine

Duchy of Brittany

County of Maine

County of Blois

County of Champagne

County of Anjou

County of Nevers

Duchy of Burgundy

County of Burgundy

Bourges

Duchy of Aquitaine

Kingdom of Burgundy and of Arles

County of Velay

Duchy of Gascony

Marquisate of Gothie

County of Provence

Kingdom of Navarre

County of Toulouse

Caliphate of Cordoba

County of Barcelona

——— Boundaries of the kingdom of France
- - - Present-day France borders
▨ King's domain
▨ Duchy of Normandy
▨ Duchy of Burgundy

SIMPLIFIED FAMILY TREE OF THE DUKES OF NORMANDY FROM 911 TO 1087

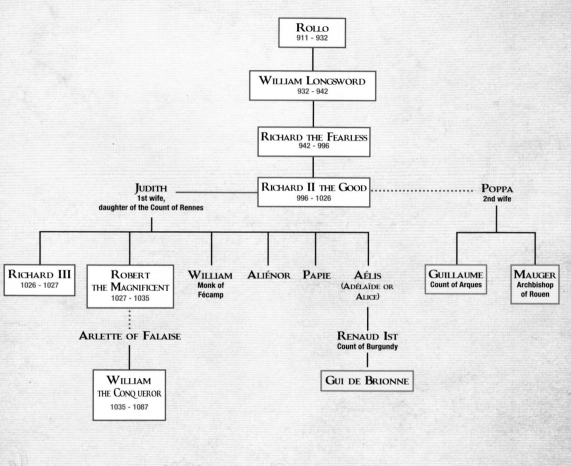

ROLLO
911 - 932

WILLIAM LONGSWORD
932 - 942

RICHARD THE FEARLESS
942 - 996

JUDITH
1st wife,
daughter of the Count of Rennes

RICHARD II THE GOOD
996 - 1026

POPPA
2nd wife

RICHARD III
1026 - 1027

ROBERT THE MAGNIFICENT
1027 - 1035

WILLIAM
Monk of
Fécamp

ALIÉNOR

PAPIE

AÉLIS
(ADÉLAÏDE OR ALICE)

GUILLAUME
Count of Arques

MAUGER
Archbishop
of Rouen

ARLETTE OF FALAISE

RENAUD IST
Count of Burgundy

WILLIAM THE CONQUEROR
1035 - 1087

GUI DE BRIONNE

DUKES OF NORMANDY
Dates of Reign

RICHARDIDES

——————— wife

············ *Frilla* (concubine)

THE DISPUTED HERITAGE

Hunted down, young William is constantly forced to flee and hide. (Still from the film *William, the Conqueror's youth*) © Les films du Cartel

In 1035, before leaving for a pilgrimage to the Holy Land, the Duke of Normandy, Robert the Magnificent, also known as "the Liberal", made arrangements to prepare the succession and guarantee the continuity of his dukedom. He organized a meeting with the Norman Barons in Fécamp and made them swear allegiance to his son William. As his boy was only 7 or 8 at that time, Robert made King Henry 1st of France protector of the province, then designated Gilbert of Brionne, a loyal baron, as the child's tutor and named Alain of Brittany as regent of the Dukedom.

"Asez li firent serement	"Thus they swore to him
Féaltez et aliement,	Loyalty and allegiance,
Ceo ke barun è vavassur	As barons and vassals are bound to do
Deivent fere à lige Seignur." (Wace)	To their liege lord. "

Robert died on his way back from pilgrimage, leaving his only son William as head of the dukedom.

From then on, all over the duchy, noble families began to wage war against each other, plunging the region into chaos. All through William's youth, the county suffered unending power struggles. These were instigated by, among others, the Richardides, Richard 1st descendants, who, being jealous of the young Duke, wanted to seize his lands, wealth and power. The pretext of William's illegitimacy was only mentioned by chroniclers much later.

> William's mother, Herlève or Arlette, was Robert the Magnificent's *Frilla*. *Frilla* is a Nordic word meaning acknowledged concubine. This officially recognized polygamy, commonly practiced in Normandy in ancient times, was known as *more danico* in Latin, or *danesche manere* in Norman, which means "the Danish way". It was common practice among Robert's ancestors, but the tradition began to be condemned by the Church whose spiritual influence was growing rapidly in Normandy.

Owing to these endless and ruthless battles, to which were added famines and epidemics, the people suffered. The young Duke himself narrowly escaped death several times. His tutor Gilbert of Brionne, was murdered by Raoul of Gace who was the son of Robert, Archbishop of Rouen, himself William's uncle (see simplified genealogical tree). His tutor Turold suffered the same fate. The Steward of the household, Osborn of Crepon was murdered in the room he shared with William in Le Vaudreuil.

Thus, throughout his youth, William was forced to live in hiding, probably under the protection of his mother's family.

The Barons Vow to Strike Against the Duke

In Bayeux, rebels swore on saintly relics to get rid of William. (Still from the film *William, the Conqueror's youth*) © Les films du Cartel

In the year 1046-1047, William was 19 years old. Over the previous four years he had governed the Duchy of Normandy. But he found it hard to impose his authority, particularly in the west of the region. Here there was little enthusiasm for obedience to "the bastard duke".

Unlike their peers in the east, who had quickly adopted French rules, these lords had retained their Scandinavian ancestors' love of freedom and independence. At that time, the viscounts had sole rule over their estates: administrative, financial, legal, religious and military. Some, not wanting to lose their powers, joined the barons in a rebellion.

Thus, several vassals of the young lord met in Bayeux and swore on saintly relics to get rid of William once and for all.

For their leader they chose Guy of Brionne, son of the count of Burgundy and grandson, on his mother's side, of Richard II. This meant he was William's cousin. William, having grown up with him, was very fond of him and, for his stronghold, had given him the estates of Vernon and Brionne. But Guy agreed to lead the conspiracy feeling that he had a legitimate right to inherit the Duchy of Normandy since William was illegitimate. The Duke had come to Valognes for hunting and business and the felons seized this opportunity to carry out their plan. William only just escaped the ambush thanks to the loyalty of his faithful fool, Golet, and reached the safety of his Falaise castle. This marked the beginning of open hostilities.

The story of the escape from Valognes is certainly historical fact, but the romanticized telling of it may not be absolutely accurate. In his *La Fuite de Valognes: comparaison des différentes versions en langue vernaculaire* (2008), Stéphane Laîné gives a detailed analysis of the events. He suggests the reason for the escape being said to have taken place at Valognes, may be found in Wace's *Roman de Rou* which was written in the 1170s. At that time, the royal court of Henri II often stayed in the ducal - turned royal- manor of Valognes when visiting the Cotentin as it was one of their frequently used residencies. In his chronicle about William of Arques' uprising (1052), William of Jumièges described how William was obliged to flee the Cotentin to reach Arques. However, the historian made a chronological inversion between the two rebellions, describing the 1052 revolt first, and then in similar terms the one against the Duke (1046 or 1047). Wace follows this version and reverses the historical facts. And, trusting to the beliefs of his time, he does not locate the event in the Cotentin but specifically in Valognes.

The rebels seized the Duke's domains. The western part of the duchy was plunged into anarchy. Lords indulged in private wars, retaliation, looting and other violent acts. The common people suffered. From then on William ruled only half of Normandy.

The motte and bailey castle at Olivet

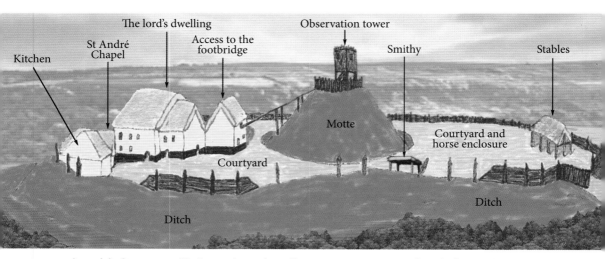

A model of a motte and bailey castle resulting from an excavation carried out by Joseph Decaën between 1976 and 79. (Publication du Centre de Recherches Archéologiques et Historiques Médiévales, Centre Michel-de-Boüard, université de Caen). © Hchc2009 Wikimedia Commons

During this time of trouble and insecurity, many lords built fortifications, to show their power or simply for protection.

It is thought that a certain Erneis, brother of Raoul Taisson, Lord of Cinglais, built a motte and bailey castle at the place called "Olivet" in around 1040-1050. At that time, relations between the two brothers were strained. We can see the superstructure of this fortification to this day in the forest of Grimbosq, eight hundred metres to the north of the Chêne Guillot car park.

THE DUKE AND THE KING GATHER THEIR TROOPS

William asks the King of France for help. (Still from the film *William, the Conqueror's youth*) © Les films du Cartel

This was too much! William hurried to Poissy to ask for help from his lord, Henri 1st, the King of France, who, according to the rules of chivalry, was bound to give him support and assistance. Remembering that William's father, Robert the Magnificent, had helped him sixteen years earlier and fearing the growing power of the lords of Burgundy, Henri agreed to help the young Duke to put down the rebellion. It was the custom in feudal times for lords to demand forty days of military service (or "service d'ost", army duty) from their vassals.

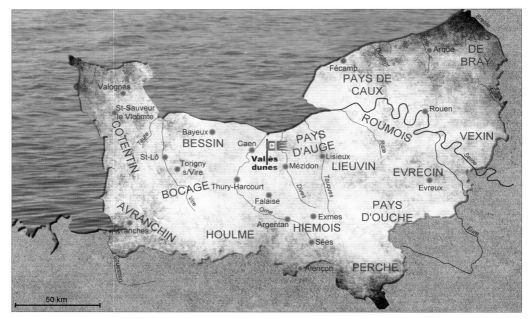

Some of the regions and towns of present day Normandy with connections to the battle.
© Jean-Paul Hauguel

> *"Et par paroles que il dit,*
> *Fit le Roi assembler son ost,*
> *En Normandie vint mult tost."* (Wace)

> *"And through the words which he said,*
> *The King assembled his army,*
> *To Normandy came a great host."*

This was a severe blow to the rebels, for the King's army was formidable. Nevertheless, they were determined to fight.

> *"Par mal cunseil ke unt créu,*
> *Epar orguil ke il unt eu,*
> *Ne li deignierent li suen rendre,*
> *Ne paiz requerre, ne paiz prendre."*
> (Wace)

> *"They gave heed to evil counsel,*
> *And in the pride of their hearts,*
> *Would not surrender,*
> *Nor ask for peace nor offer it."*

They recruited family, friends, vassals and all those who had sworn to fight by their side.

The Camp at Argences. (Still from the film *William, the Conqueror's youth*) © Les films du Cartel

Thus, in that summer of 1047, two armies prepared to do battle. From those counties which had remained loyal to him, William called up his fighters; knights who owed him service in times of war.

<table>
<tr><td>

"E Willame semont Cauchoiz,
Cels de Roem è de Roumoiz,
E la gent d'Auge è de Liévin,
E cels d'Evreus è d'Evrecin." (Wace)

</td><td>

"William summons the Cauchois,
Those from Rouen and from Roumois,
And the troops from Pays d'Auge and Lieuvin,
And those from Evreux and Evrecin."

</td></tr>
</table>

Benoît of Sainte-Maure adds those from Sées, Falaise and Hiémois (Exmes region). Jean Nagerel (Mésigier publishing, XVIth/XVIIth century) adds the people of Caen alongside William. According to William of Poitiers, Rouen refuses to march with the young Duke.

William established his camp at Argences, a good place from which to await reinforcements from the King's army, which he knew was not far off.

The centre of the market town of Argences bears the hallmarks of an ancient *oppidum* (Iron Age fortified settlement) situated opposite the ford which allowed travelers coming from the Pays d'Auge to cross the River Muance. The estate had belonged to Fécamp Abbey since 990 when Duke Richard the 1st had made a settlement of it which was then renewed in 1025 by his son, Richard the 2nd, William's grandfather. When William made camp there he was,

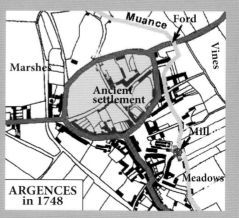

therefore, in allied country, in the stronghold of the Abbot of Fécamp. When we realise the strong bonds which had linked the Duke's family and Fécamp Abbey for decades we can more easily understand that the lord of the estate would be a loyal vassal. The village had possessed a market place and a mill for at least twenty years. There William could get fresh supplies for his men and find all they needed: pasture, cereals and flour, wine, wood... It was a good base camp.

The King had put out the bans of war and called his vassals to his banner. At the head of his army he arrived in Normandy, passing through the county of Hiémois. At that time, when going to or from the Ile de France it was preferable to go through the Exmes-Argentan region rather than the Pays d'Auge. Then he headed north to Argences where William was waiting for him.

The King's troops camped near the River Laizon at Mézidon, probably at the Ouézy forge and at Canon where Odon Stigand also stayed. Stigand had been close to Robert the Magnificent, accompanying him to the Holy Land, and also to William for whom he was the steward.

"Entre Argence et Mezodon *Sor la rivière de Lizon* *Se hébergerent cil de France."* (Wace)	*"Between Argences and Mézidon* *Over the River of Laizon* *Camped the men of France."*

Around 1050, on Duke William's orders, Odon Stigand had a fortress built at a strategic spot on the banks of the River Dives, which became the center of a new barony; from that fortress the village of Mézidon grew, whose name in Mediaeval Latin is Mansione Odonis which means "The domain of Odon".

"E li reis fu jà tant allez *Od ses granz osz démesurez* *Que sus l'Eison, ès prez herbuz,* *Près d'Arverenches sunt descenduz;* *Là furent les granz osts logées,* *Là firent loges et foilliées."* (Benoît de Sainte-Maure)	*"And the King had travelled so far* *With his immeasurable armies* *That by the River Laizon, in the grassy* *meadows,* *Near Argences they stayed;* *There were the great armies lodged,* *There they built huts and fires."*

These "grassy meadows" were important for in the 11th century armies on campaign did not carry fodder for the horses (nor reserves of food for the men).

For their part, the rebels had crossed the River Orne at several fords, which was the method of crossing at the time. Upriver of Caen there were many fords: Athis (at Fleury-sur-Orne/Allemagne), Fontenay (at Saint-André-sur-Orne), Bully (where the famous Roman road linking Bayeux to Exmes via Vieux crossed the River Orne), Le Coudray (at Amayé-sur-Orne), Brye (at Goupillières)…

On the morning of the battle the rebels set off for Val ès dunes where they were to regroup.

Val ès dunes is in Hiemois

NORTH-WEST

Sequeville Malcouronne Saint-Laurent hill Caen (12 km) Chichebovill

The Val ès dunes plain. © Photo Olivier Hauguel

The lords of Sequeville planted Scot's pines on the hills surrounding Val ès dunes at the beginning of the 19th century. © Photo Jean-Paul Hauguel

Val ès dunes lies twelve kilometres to the south east of Caen, between the D 613 and the N 158 roads, south easterly from the D 41 which goes from Bellengreville to Secqueville. It is a small valley nestling between Secqueville and Chicheboville. You must imagine a rather different landscape than that of today. If now the slopes are covered with Scots pines, in those days the soil was not suitable for cultivation and the hills were practically bare. The beginning of the 11th century was marked by an important shift in the demography, economy and even the cultural life of the community. Agriculture became more important as shown by the increasing number of mills to be found in the area at that time. The nearby plain which slopes towards the east was therefore probably cultivated and its aspects would have been similar to that of today with "no copse nor rock".

It would seem that the explanation of the place name could be drawn from the words val – valley – between the dunes – heights - , which seems obvious when we look at the geography of the place. But nothing is certain in historical interpretation, least of all an 'obvious' explanation. In 2010, Professor Dominique Fournier (a specialist in medieval linguistics) suggested that the name comes from 'Dunes' meaning heights, preceded by a mediaeval family name Waleis, ie The heights of Waleis. This name, which occurs frequently in the old Norman language, became Galeis in Old French, then Galois (Gallois from Pays de Galles, ie: Wales).
The name was reinterpreted as valley in the dunes quite late on (there is no clear form of this popular etymology before the 16th century). In the 11th century, Val ès dunes was therefore Waleis Heights.

"Valesdune est en Oismeiz
Entre Argences è Cinguelaeiz ;
De Caen on peut l'en compter
Trois lieues à mien kuider:
Les plaines sont longues et lées,
N'y a grands monts ni grandes vallées,
Assez proche du gué Bérangier,
N'y a bocage ne rocher,
Mais encontre soleil levant
Se fond la terre en avalant ;
Une rivière l'avirone
Deverz midi et deverz none." (Wace)

"Val ès dunes is in Hiemois,
Between Argences and the Cinglais forest;
From Caen, to my reckoning
Three leagues we can count:
The plains are vast and broad,
No true hill nor valley,
Not far from the Beranger ford,
There is no wood nor grove,
But when facing the rising sun
The earth slopes gently into the distance;
One river bounds it
Towards the south and towards noon."

In the liturgy, noon is at 3 pm, which designates south west. In the poem noon means south, because there is no river located to the south-west. Wace no doubt chose that word for the rhyme, without thinking geographically. For his part, Benoît de Sainte-Maure speaks only of a river to the south: *"Straight towards noon in such a way/It is bordered by a river"*.

Why did the battle take place at Val ès dunes? In those days, Val ès dunes was a strategic location situated at the crossroads of two major highways: one between Vieux and Lisieux through the Berenger Ford on the Semillon river (near Vimont and Bellengreville), the other between Caen and Exmes (towards the Jort bridges). A third route was the salt road from north to south. Whoever held the Berenger ford held the access to the Pays d'Auge and the west of Normandy. But due to the lie of the land around the ford, a battle here would have been quite impossible. However, nearby there was a plain where the knights could manoeuver. The choice of the ground for the battle was probably tacitly accepted by both sides. In the light of the new ideas of chivalry, battles were rather like a joust, a divine judgment, a challenge or duel mutually agreed upon.

The Berenger Ford

The Berenger Ford, called vey Berenger, vey Bellenger or gué Berenger, takes its name from a certain Berengarius, of German origin, which also gives us the name of the town: Bellengreville.

Lucien Musset, in his study published in le *Bulletin de la Société des Antiquaires de Normandie* (April 4th, 1959) revealed the importance of the ford through the powder tax that was levied there. This remnant of an old roman tax probably dates from the 12th century. Up to the revolution the tax was still levied on the inhabitants of the parishes of Secqueville-la-Champaigne, Saint-Laurent-du-Val-ès-dunes, the Croix-Cornet (crossroad of the ancient ways on the Val ès dunes, called the Croix-Caunet in recent documents), the Vey Bellenger, Vimont, Moult, Ingouville, Frénouville, Esmiéville and Chicheboville. The inhabitants of these parishes were also responsible for policing the ford. The tax was collected each year, on Saint Jean-Baptiste day (June 24th) during the fair, for over four centuries from the 11th to the 15th century or even later. This tax was then given to the royal treasury on Saint Michael's day (September 29th).

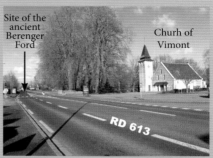

Site of the ancient Berenger ford, on the RD 613 between Vimont and Bellengreville
© Photo Jean-Paul Hauguel

The Berenger Ford was of importance for a long period of time. It is represented on ancient maps: the map of the diocese of Lisieux, ordered by the bishop M. de Branca and the map of Guillaume Mariette de la Pagerie (see p-20). Up to 1735, the ford was the only way to cross the River Semillon. The ford was replaced by a small bridge when the Great Royal Way (the curent D 613) was built under Louis the XVth. Even now, it is still a very important thoroughfare as we can see by the traffic jams.

On the commemorative pillar which Arcisse de Caumont had erected by the side of the D 613 at Vimont, he mistakenly placed the ford on the River Muance: "The Duke crossed the Muance at the Berenger Ford near Argences".

A precise date for the battle has been given by 19th century historians: that of August the 10th 1047. Even if no ancient documents provide clear proof, it is convenient and maybe useful. August the 10th is Saint Laurent's day. According to some historians, William had a chapel built in commemoration of his victory, on top of Saint Laurent's hill, at the place where the outcome of the battle was decided.

When erecting a sanctuary on the site of his victory, William followed the example of other winners. These foundations are acts of penance for the blood shed in battle and a way to commemorate a victory. This will happen in 1066. After the Battle of Hastings, William will erect the Battle Abbey on the site of the battle.

However, an archeological excavation in 1868 revealed that a commemorative chapel had been erected using the remains of an ancient church which had stood nearby. In a statement given in 1870 to the antiquary society of Normandy, about the Saint-Laurent church, the Abbot Noel declared: "*Any confusion between the Chapel and the Church of Saint-Laurent is now at an end [after the discovery] and the old tradition and beliefs strongly confirmed.*" There was an ancient church dedicated to Saint-Laurent probably before the 11th century. Dedications to this saint had been made early in the history of Christianity. Thus it cannot be stated with certainty that the battle took place on August the 10th.

At 1km north-east of the church at Vimont, the Brasier Ford on the same River Sémillon gives an idea of what the Berenger Ford would have been like before 1735. © Photo Jean-Paul Hauguel

In 1868, excavations were carried out at Saint-Laurent's hill, and two remnants of old churches were found. One was 23 metres long and 6.6 metres wide and housed Merovingian graves. The other was only 6 metres long and 5 metres wide. The first one was the old church of Saint Laurent's parish. The small one, built with the fallen stones of the previous one, was raised to commemorate William's victory. It is well know that monuments built to commemorate battles are small.

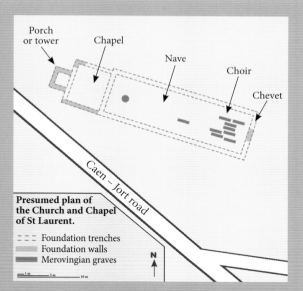

Presumed plan of the Church and Chapel of St Laurent.

≡ ≡ ≡ Foundation trenches
░░░ Foundation walls
▓▓▓ Merovingian graves

Presumed plan of the Church and Chapel of Saint-Laurent. © Jean-Paul Hauguel

According to M. de Bras (*Recherches et Antiquitez de la ville de Caen*), the chapel had been built on the top of Val ès dunes, and dedicated to Saint Laurent in memory of the dead. This chapel was destroyed by Protestants in the year 1562.

Nevertheless, we know that those who fled the battle passed through fields of 'bled' or 'wheat' (Old French). That this detail was still remembered one hundred and twenty years after the battle would seem to indicate that the wheat was not young. The harvest could take place from the beginning of july or mid-September at the latest depending on the weather. Besides, the need for grass to feed the horses obliged the combatants to fight between April and September. The only thing we can say, therefore, without fear of contradiction, is that the Val ès dunes battle took place during the summer of 1047.

The troops enter Val ès dunes

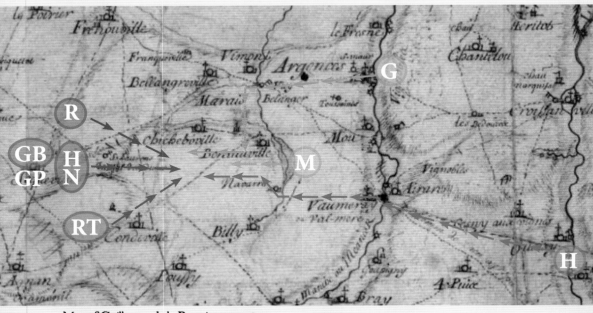

Map of Guillaume de la Pagerie - 1720 © BNF

G = Guillaume (William)	R = Ranulf, Viscount of Bessin	GB = Gui of Brionne
H = Henri Ist of France	H = Hamon le dentu	GP = Grimout of Plessis
M = People's militias	N = Néel II, Viscount of Cotentin	RT = Raoul Taisson of Cinglais

"It was a fine morning" Benoît of Sainte-Maure declared later.

In the early morning of that beautiful summer's day 1047, the French troops left their camps on the River Laizon, reached Airan and crossed the River Muance at Valmeray, where King Henri attended Mass in the Church of Saint-Brice. Meanwhile the troops were organized into squadrons and put on their armour before moving off towards Val ès dunes. Nowadays, a path leading from Valmeray to Béneauville is called "the King's Way". Is it the one King Henri took that day?

"A Saint-Briçun de Valmerei
Fut la messe chantée el Rei
Li jor ke la bataille fu ;
Grant poor y unt li cler éu.
A Valmerei Franceiz s'armèrent,
E lor batailles ordonnerent,
Puiz entrerent à Valesdunes." (Wace)

"At Saint- Brice de Valmeray
The Mass had been sung to the King
The battle took place that very day ;
Great fear seized upon all the clerics.
At Valmeray the French took their arms,
And their troops got into order,
Then they entered Val ès dunes."

La Tour de Valmeray (classified site - photo Pierre Leroy, collection Lucienne Couffin-Duppéron) at the beginning of the 20th century and after its restoration in 2010. It was here that Henri Ist, King of France, heard Mass on the morning of the battle.

Depending on the precise day of the battle (between July the 1st and September the 30th), the sun would have risen between 4 and 6 AM. As dawn is three-quarters of an hour before sun-rise, the King and his army would have had enough time to march the twelve kilometres to the Val ès dunes battlefield.

On the morning of October the 14th 1066, William the conqueror's troops marched eleven kilometres from Hastings to the battlefield (now called Battle) before getting fully equipped for the fight.

> *"Jà esteit bien prime passée."*   ***"The hour of Prime was long past."***
>   (Benoît of Sainte-Maure)
>
> As Prime is said at the first canonical hour (6 am), and six o'clock is already long gone, this means the battle could have taken place around 9 or 10 am.

William had more time than the King, having only eight kilometres to march. In Argences he also woke up very early. Wace tells us he made the sign of the cross before leaving.

We can assume he attended Mass in the monks' chapel at Argences and his men in Saint-Patrice's parish church. He gave his orders, put on his armour and went to the head of his troops.

His army followed what is now the Vimont road, reached the Berenger Ford and marched up river to the plain between Beneauville and Chicheboville to join the French.

> *"Willame, d'Argences torna,*
> *Par le vé Beranger passa,*
> *Amont la rivière est alé,*
> *Tant k'il est as Franceiz josté."* (Wace)

> *"William from Argences moved,*
> *Passed at Berenger Ford*
> *And marched upriver*
> *To join the French army."*

> *"D'Argences se parti li dux,*
> *De rien ne se ratarga plus ;*
> *Le heaume lacié, sor le destrer,*
> *Passa sor le gué Berenger,*
> *Od sa bone gent armée*
> *Que il r'out partie et sevrée,*
> *Preste de traire e de lancier*
> *E de ferir des branz d'acier."*
> (Benoît of Sainte-Maure)

> *"Duke William from Argences went,*
> *Nothing could stop him;*
> *His nasal helmet tightly laced, on his steed,*
> *He went across the Berenger ford,*
> *With his strong army fully equipped,*
> *That he had organized and commanded,*
> *Ready to throw spears and arrows*
> *And to strike with swords of steel."*

The troops recruited from the common people, peasants with pitch forks, scythes and clubs, had gathered alongside the Semillon River, between Béneauville and Navarre where they stood, waiting for King Henri and Duke William's armies.

> *"La s'asemblerent li cumunes,*
> *Tutes propistrent la rivière,*
> *Bien cunréez come gent fiere."* (Wace)

> *"Here (at Val ès dunes) gathered the peasants' militia*
> *On either side of the river,*
> *Carrying their weapons proudly."*

The Duke and the King proceeded together towards the west.

As for the rebels they marched about twelve kilometres from the banks of the River Orne, which they also had left early that morning or even the day before, to gather at Val ès dunes.

> *"Oune unt passée od comunes,*
> *Dreit sunt venu en Valesdunes."*
> (Benoît of Sainte-Maure)

> *"They crossed the river Orne*
> *With their troops of yeomen*
> *And marched straight to Val ès dunes."*

Such Great Armies Are Going To Fight

On the plain of Val ès dunes, battle is about to begin. We must imagine, as well as foot soldiers, many squadrons of knights drawn up on ground which is more open, more suitable for cavalry. (Still from the film *William, the Conqueror's youth*) © Les films du Cartel

William's Normans were positioned on the right flank of the French. Both armies faced towards the west. Straight towards them came the rebels.

"La gent Willame fu à destre, *E Franceiz furent à senestre ;* *Verz ocidenttornent lor vis,* *Quer là sourent les anemis."* (Wace)	*"William's army was to the right,* *The French were to the left;* *Turned their faces to the west* *From where their enemies advanced."*

Among the rebel armies, that from the Bessin, commanded by Ranulf of Briquessard, the Viscount of Bayeux, was drawn up to the north of William's troops. The troops from Cotentin, more numerous than the Bessin army and led by Néel the 2nd, Viscount of St-Sauveur, stood to the right of them facing the French (according to Benoît of Sainte-Maure), along with Hamon le Dentu, baron of Thorigny and Creully. Benoît of Sainte-Maure called the latter the anti-Christ. A contingent led by Gui of Brionne had joined the rebels. If they won the battle it was he who would become the Duke of Normandy. At the end of the battle, Benoît positions him next to the Cotentins, there-

(Still from the film *William, the Conqueror's youth*) © Les films du Cartel

fore opposite the French. We don't know the position of Grimout of Plessis, a very wealthy nobleman who owned 10,000 hectares (24,710 acres) to the north of Condé-en-Normandie. Stéphane Laîné observes that he had stakes in the lands close to the battle (Ifs, Hubert-Folie, Allemagne…). According to Wace he had a bad reputation, was hated by all and served the Duke only grudgingly. Benoît de Sainte-Maure compares him to the traitor Ganelon who caused the death of Roland at Roncevaux.

On the right side of the rebels, a group of men was waiting and watching: it was the army of Raoul the 2nd of Taisson, lord of Cinglais, one of the richest land owners in Normandy. From his vantage point he can see the growing numbers of the French and Norman armies as they march onto the plain. The Duke and the King are all the more visible since:

> *"En mi lor vis vers occident*
> *Resplendi cler l'or e l'argent*
> *Des armes à lor enemis."*

> *"Turning their faces to the west,*
> *Their weapons of gold and silver*
> *Dazzle their enemies."*

Gold and silver weapons, a fine exaggeration by Benoît of Sainte-Maure!

Holding their commanders' batons, the King and William get their troops into battle order.

Baton in hand, William leads his army.
© Bayeux Tapestry - the 11th century, with special permission from the City of Bayeux

Chroniclers and historians have said that the rebel army numbered between 20,000 and 30,000 men and that of the King, 10,000. These figures are no doubt exaggerations. Benoît of Sainte-Maure writes that William was surrounded by three hundreds knights "wearing nasal helmets". Wace tells

LOYALISTS	KNIGHTS	INFANTRY	TOTAL
William	110	440	550
Henri	190	760	950
Total	**300**	**1200**	**1500**

RALLIED TO THE CAUSE	KNIGHTS	INFANTRY	TOTAL
Raoul Taisson	45	180	225

REBELS	KNIGHTS	INFANTRY	TOTAL
Grimoult	40	160	200
Hamon le Dentu	35	140	175
Néel	30	120	150
Ranulf	30	120	150
Gui of B. + div.	35	140	175
Total	**170**	**680**	**850**

us that Raoul Taisson is accompanied by one hundred and forty knights, while Benoît quotes one hundred. But Michel de Boüard thought that he had around forty-five. This hypothesis is compatible with Philippe Contamine's study covering this period, which notes that, in the area of Cinglais alone, where Raoul was lord, there were three or four castles and twenty-eight mottes or keeps (among them that of Raoul's brother, Erneis. Therefore, counting the other knights from round about, we can indeed surmise that Raoul's company numbered about forty-five knights. In the light of his own research, Thierry Wavelet suggests the breakdown set out below. Comparing it with other battles of the same period it would seem to be accurate.

At the start of the battle there were therefore, theoretically, 1,100 on the rebels' side and 1,500 with the loyalists. Counting the chargers for replacing fallen mounts, the palfreys or light saddle horses and the cart horses used for transportation, it is estimated that around 1,000 horses were to be found gathered on the battle field.

THE WHOLE EARTH SHAKES AND TREMBLES

"Dex aïe !" (Still from the film *William, the Conqueror's youth*) © Les films du Cartel

Having divided their groups of knights into squadrons of thirty or forty each led by a captain, the King and the Duke mounted at their head. It was mid-morning. Battle was about to begin when William and Henri saw a detachment of knights arriving from their left. It was Raoul of Taisson and some of his men, advancing towards them, with obviously peaceful intentions. Previously, at Bayeux, in front of several viscounts, Raoul had sworn that he would strike

William as soon as he saw him, wherever that might be. But his men had insisted that during the battle he must show respect to his sovereign lord. Raoul halted his men someway off and approached the young duke alone. He struck William with his glove. Wace recounts what happened next:

"Poiz li a tot en riant dit:
De ço ke jo jurai m'aquit;
Jo jurai ke jo vos ferreie
Si tost com jo vos trovereie;
Por mon serement aquiter,
Quer jo ne me voil perjurer,
Vos ai féru ne vos poist mie
Ne faiz por altre félunie,
E li Dus dist: Vostre merci,
E Raol atant s'en parti." (Wace)

"Then laughing he said:
I have kept my oath;
I swore I would strike you
As soon as I found you;
To be true to my word,
For I would not perjure myself,
I struck you, be not angry
I will do you no other wrong.
And the Duke said: I give thee thanks.
And Raoul went away."

This was a great disappointment to the barons.

The loyalist armies continued their advance towards the rebels. It was a beautiful morning. At about 10 o'clock the battle began.

We can imagine that, like most battles, this one began with the enemies hurling insults at each other from their respective sides. We would have heard *"apresmiez farrains!"* (come here, you animals!), *"culverz!"* (traitor!), *"ecouilles!"* (cullions), *"fitz hore"* (whoreson!) etc.. (cf "membres.lycos.fr/hagdik/Hastings2000/Insultes")

All through the battle men were shouting their war cries. This was both to give themselves courage and also as a means of recognizing each other for at that time there were no uniforms or coats of arms as these only appeared in the second half of the 12th century. The French battle cry was *"Mountjoy!"* and *"Saint Denis!"*, that of William's men *"Deix Aïe"* ("God be our help". It is the motto of Normandy); the war cry of Néel's men from the Cotentin was *"Saint-Sauveur!"*, the people of Bayeux *"Saint-Sever!"*, Hamon's men *"Saint Amant"* and those with Raoul *"Tur Aie!"* (which gives us 'Thury', the name of the town of which he was the sovereign).

Then the archers let fly their arrows. As the tight shot bows' range was about fifty metres we must assume they were quite close to enemy lines. The onslaught would have lasted for some time as each side fired back the arrows that fell among them.

Finally the cavalry began to manoeuver and attack each other in furious charges. William went cross country. He was resolute. His future and his life itself depend on the outcome of this battle. He led a large company of Normans and hunted for the two viscounts and traitors. Those who spotted them pointed them out to him. Everywhere knights and captains, horsemen and groups of men on foot were fighting each other. The cries of men and terrified horses were deafe-

In the 11th century the Norman bow which was quite small (1,30 metre) gave little force of penetration. It was a simple curved bow made out of yew. When fired in a high trajectory the arrows can travel more than 150 metres. © Bayeux Tapestry - the 11th century, with special permission from the City of Bayeux

ning. The noise was so great that it drowned out the clashing of weapons or the thundering of hooves that made the ground tremble. Nothing could be seen save for a dense cloud of dust pierced by flashes of light, out of which rose the groans and cries of triumph or of agony, the whinnying of horses, the clamor of attack or retreat.

"Dux Guillaumes, li genz, li proz,
Qui al ovraigne entent sor toz,
Kar bien seit e veit senz dotance
Qu'iloc est tote sa chaance
Ou d'estre riche e honorez
Ou d'estre vis deserite..."
(Benoît of Sainte-Maure)

"Duke William, the faithful, the gallant,
Is fighting to succeed,
For he sees without doubt
That here lies his destiny
Either to be rich and honoured
Or to find himself destitute..."

On the left flank of the loyalists, the French, after several attempts, succeeded in making a breech in the Cotentin lines. At the height of the battle a Cotentin knight charged at the King of France and knocked him from his horse. The King, unharmed, climbed back on his horse and carried on fighting more fiercely than ever. His assailant was at once surrounded by several French knights who toppled him from his mount and he died under their horses' trampling hooves. This deed was later associated with a place nearby which becomes known as "Malcouronne", the site where the crown was brought down.

The foot soldiers armour consisted of a spear about 2.20 metres long, a battle axe or a round ended sword used only for slashing and cutting, the piercing action with the point only coming into use in the 13th century. A kite shaped shield about 1.20 metre tall, protects him from the shoulder to the feet and in its centre there is an 'umbo' or boss which can absorb or deflect blows. It is painted and decorated but has no display of heraldry, this only appearing on armour in the second half of the 12th century.

Some infantrymen continue to carry round shields. They also wear gloves in battle. However in the middle of the 11th century few foot soldiers are so well equipped. The picture above is more likely to be of a horseman who has dismounted, a common practice of the time to enable him to command his men. Armour did not yet exist; to protect themselves, fighters wear ring mail (a type of coat on which are sewn together metallic rings or overlapping scales, depending on the wealth of the owner), a neck protection and a nasal helm, which was often painted. The heaviest equipment does not weigh more than 15kg.

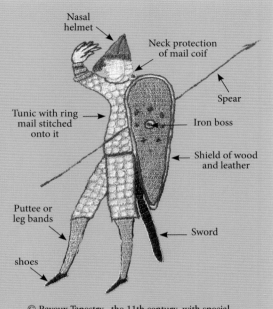

Nasal helmet

Neck protection of mail coif

Spear

Tunic with ring mail stitched onto it

Iron boss

Shield of wood and leather

Puttee or leg bands

Sword

shoes

© Bayeux Tapestry - the 11th century, with special permission from the City of Bayeux

Malcouronne is a hill just south-east of the electricity station at La Tourbe (D 41). In fact, this place name could be associated with the nick-name for a badly tonsured monk "badly crowned". Was it used to describe this hill, which might have been dotted with bushes much as we see it today, because it looked like a badly shaven monk's head? Whatever the truth, this feat of arms lingered in the popular imagination one century later, in these few lines by Benoît de Sainte-Maure:

> *"Ne sai qui fu le chevalier ;*
> *Mais de Costentin vint la lance*
> *Qui abati le rei de France."*

> *"No one knows who was the knight*
> *But from Cotentin came the spear*
> *Which toppled the King of France."*

At the height of battle, having been struck down from his horse, the King of France is lifted up by his men. (Still from the film *William, the Conqueror's youth*) © Les films du Cartel

Then the King and his troops led a ferocious attack against Hamon and his men. Hamon fell, mortally wounded, and was found dead, lying on his shield. His body was carried to Esquay-sur-Seulles, 6 km to the east of Bayeux, and was buried under the parvis of the church. Many knights from his estate and family suffered the same fate.

At the height of the battle Raoul made up his mind to fight with... the loyalists. It would be impossible to count his brave deeds that day. The rebels were now seriously outnumbered!

During a battle a Norman horseman would ride a small stallion (1.45 metre - 1.50 metres high at the withers) similar to a cob. Wealthy noblemen may have had swifter, Mediterranean horses. In the 11th century, Norman horsemen were superior to other fighters when it came to equestrian battles for they were skilled and had cutting-edge equipment. The wrap

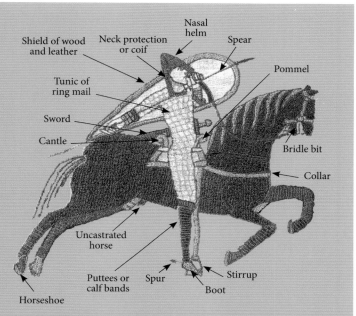

A knight's equipment in the 11th century. © Bayeux Tapestry - the 11th century, with special permission from the City of Bayeux

around saddle with its high pommel in front and cantle behind gave stability, while the long stirrups, the bridle and the girth all helped the cavalier to charge with his spear held horizontal for power and precision, though in this illustration it is held high like a javelin. He also has his kite-shaped shield, of about 1.20 metre in height, which he carries in his left hand along with the reins. The Normans successfully adopted the horse shoe, spurs and bridle bit. In battle they group themselves into *conrois* or squadrons of about 20 or 30 horsemen who charge head on in two or three ranks. The captain of a conroi carried a piece of cloth fixed to the head of his spear - an ensign, so that he can be recognized. These squadrons were known for their discipline and were considered to be the backbone of the Norman armies.

According to Wace, some knights would attach a small piece of taffeta to the shaft of their spear, a silken token given to them by their sweetheart for good luck.

On the right of the battlefield William had no choice as to what tactics to use. With a marsh and the foot of a hill to his right and the French troops to his left he had no alternative but to attack the enemy head on. The hail of arrows and the cavalry charges alternated, each bringing their toll of dead and wounded. Then followed indescribable hand to hand combat. Some later said there were so many fighting that the dead had no room to fall! A slight exaggeration perhaps!

At the head of his troops William fought like a lion. The 'gallant' and 'chivalrous' knight outdid everyone in bravery. Surrounded by his horsemen, wearing his gleaming helmet, he was to be seen everywhere. He recognized Ranulf and was about to attack him when a man from Bayeux, a knight called Hardré, stepped in to protect his lord. He aimed a blow at the Duke with his spear which the latter parried with his shield. In his turn, William struck and pierced the man through the neck with his own dagger, killing him on the spot. Leaving his dagger embedded in the dead man's throat, William grasped his sword and with it defeated many other enemies.

A Conroi. © Éditions Harnois 84400 APT (Hastings 2000)

William fights like a lion. *(Still from the film* William, the Conqueror's youth) *© Les films du Cartel*

Ranulf began to panic. His bravest knights were falling all around him on this bloody battlefield. Unable to see his ally, Néel, he feared that the knight had given up. Frozen to the spot he thought of his fate if he were to be captured – to finish on the gallows. Taking advantage of a final charge by his men, he rid himself of his weapons and rode flat out away from the battle.

Néel learned of Ranulf's desertion but continued to fight valiantly, giving courage to his men. Wace wrote that because of Néel's valour, his skill, his bravery and his nobility he was known as 'Chief of Hawks' 'Hawk's Head'. This may have been Wace's attempt to give a noble origin to a nickname which could have been bestowed simply because the knight had an aquiline profile. Having made several fruitless attacks, with the wounded continuing to fall and the deserters fleeing, Néel at last left the battlefield with great regret.

This was the signal for a general rout among the rebels. It was somewhere between eleven and midday.

Image symbolizing William having defeated Ranulf.
(Still from the film *William, the Conqueror's youth*)
© Les films du Cartel

West

Athis Farm

Former Athis Ford

Towards Caen

Orne

Rebels' attempted escape route

© Photo Jean-Paul Hauguel

Filled with panic they fled. Spurring their horses, knights fled through fields of wheat. The rebel infantry, defeated, escaped in little groups of three, five, six. Some tried to reach safety on the other side of the River Orne. They were soon caught by the victors who showed no mercy and slaughtered them all. Those who could tried to cross the Orne at the Athis Ford, at Allemagne (This was what Fleury-sur-Orne was called up until the 12th of April 1917.) But it was high tide and at that time the effect of the tide could be felt as far as Fontenay Abbey, four kilometres upriver from the Athis Ford. Large numbers of those fleeing were slain on the banks of the river or swallowed by the rushing waters.

There were so many bodies that the Bourbillon water mill at Fleury (now known as the 'Île Enchantée') was blocked. In the evening the people of Caen saw the waters of the river flowing crimson.

For the rebels it was a total disaster. Their dead were numerous.

Fleury s/Orne church

East

L'Île enchantée
(formerly
Bourbillon Mill)

Towards Caen

West

River Orne

© DR

As the vassals' obligation to fight for their lord only lasted for forty days, the King made haste to take them back to l'Île-de-France, to avoid having to pay them for more time. This is what Wace tells us, explaining that, as soon as the battle ended, the King gathered his men together to return to his own lands, taking the sick and wounded with them. He adds:

"En terre efoent les ociz
As cimetieres del païz."

"They buried their dead
In the local cemetries."

Between 1867 and 1879, in the valley of Conteville where La Sablonette is situated, two cemeteries were discovered close together and they were excavated. One, in the upper part of the field to the east, where the substratum is composed of limestone was an ancient Merovingian cemetery. The other, in the lower part to the west with a substratum of white sand (easier to dig) contained

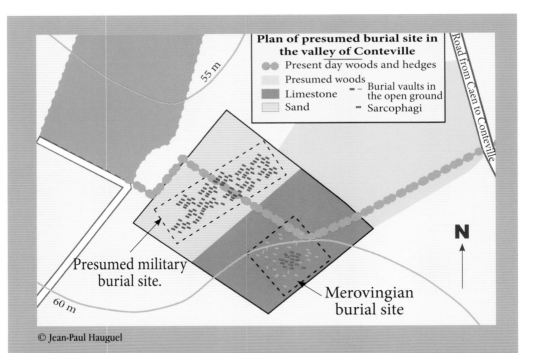

Plan of presumed burial site in the valley of Conteville

- ●● Present day woods and hedges
- Presumed woods
- Limestone
- Sand
- ‑ ‑ Burial vaults in the open ground
- = Sarcophagi

55 m

60 m

Road from Caen to Conteville

Presumed military burial site.

Merovingian burial site

N

© Jean-Paul Hauguel

tombs which were believed to be military. The latter consisted of several graves which each contained between two and six bodies buried together at a depth of around 70 cm. From a total surface of 1500 m², sixty-four skeletons were found, not counting those which remained in the rubble. With those buried in the same fashion nearby, it brought to one hundred and four the number of people interred there. According to two doctors who were working on the archeological dig, they were males aged between fifteen and sixty save for one female (unsurprising in those days). They had all been buried at the same time and, unlike in the nearby Merovingian cemetery, they had no accessories - jewelry, weapons etc.. Thanks to the Bayeux Tapestry, we know that it was traditional to strip the dead as they lay on the battlefield, taking clothes, weapons and protective garb which were very expensive. All these indications lead us to believe that these were indeed the graves of some of the dead of the Battle of Val ès dunes. Michel de Boüard has also located a mediaeval cemetery near the church at Fleury. The rebels slain on the banks of the Orne may have been buried there.

On the eve of the Battle of Hastings, the winners strip the corpses to collect the clothes, and mainly weapons and protections. © Bayeux Tapestry - the 11th century, with special permission from the City of Bayeux

The number of dead from this battle was no doubt lower than that reported later. If we consider that the total number of combatants was between 2,200 and 2,500 then it is hard to imagine that on the evening after the battle the dead lay in their thousands, as William of Malmesbury leads us to believe. Philippe Contamine in *War in the Middle Ages* tells us that the deaths resulting from war at that time were few: for example at Brémule in 1119, out of nine hundred knights, only three were slain. In proportion to the number of soldiers fighting at the battle of Val ès dunes, the death toll appears very high – which could account for the exaggeration in the numbers – but in reality it probably led to 'only' a few hundred victims (three, four, five hundred?)

WILLIAM IS NOW THE PEACEMAKER

The interior of the Church of Sainte-Paix. © Pascal Radigue Wikimedia Commons

William had a chapel built to Saint-Laurent at the highest point of the battle-field, (Saint-Laurent's Mound) there where the outcome of the fight was traditionally thought to have been decided.

Gui of Burgundy took refuge in his castle at Brionne which the Duke laid siege to for three long years. Managing to obtain satisfactory conditions from William, he finally capitulated and returned to Burgundy.

Grimoult du Plessis, who was considered to be the instigator of the rebellion, was arrested and imprisoned at Rouen, where he was to die, strangled, in his jail. Some of his property was given to Bayeux Cathedral. Some sources date his death thirty years or so after the battle.

Néel was exiled for a while and then returned to his lands. Ranulf may also have been exiled but he was pardoned.

Hamon le Dentu had his property confiscated. Nineteen years later his son, Robert Fitz-Hamon, took part in the battle of Hastings and William restored his barony to him as a reward.

"Happy battle wherein fell so many castles" a historian said later.

"E gloriose la bataille	*"And glorious was that battle*
(Ce puet-l'om bien dire senz faille),	*(We can say no less)*
Où tant out plaissié felonie	*Where so much treachery was overcome*
Par qu'ert destruite Normendie,	*That had ruined Normandy,*
Dunt tant hautes tors kernelées,	*So many battlements and towers,*
Tantes motes en haut levées,	*So many keeps and fortifications,*
Tant recet fort, tante palice	*So many strongholds, so many palisades*
E tant chastel plein de malice	*And so many castles full of wickedness*
Fu abatu e trébuché,	*Were overthrown that day and brought low,*
Dunt li regnes fu apaisié."	*Thus the country came to peace."*
(Benoît of Sainte-Maure)	

Obviously the strongholds of the traitors were not destroyed on the same day that the battle was fought. They would be demolished later.

Nevertheless the young Duke's authority was secure following this victory. Immediately, William declared the Truce of God.

At that time, the Truce of God was a relatively common practice throughout the Christian world. It forbade making war from Wednesday evening until Monday morning, as well as from the start of Advent up to Epiphany (forty days), from the beginning of Lent up to Easter (forty-eight days) from the start of Rogation until Pentecost (twenty-one days), which left around eighty to one hundred days a year for waging war. In addition, war was seldom fought in winter. Enough to discourage the most bellicose!

In addition, William imposed 'the Peace of God' which permanently protected clerics, peasants and merchants.

In October of that year, on Saint Denis Day, William called all his vassals together in Caen to have them swear loyalty to him and obedience to these laws.

Brionne Castle was built at the end of the 11th century. The location of this keep would originate a siege-castle built by William during the siege of the motte and bailey then located on an island in the river Risle.

The Church of Sainte-Paix, rue du Marais, Caen.
© Photo Jean-Paul Hauguel

They took their oaths on the New Testament and on the relics of Saint Ouen which had been brought from Rouen for the occasion. On the spot where the ceremony had taken place William had the Church of All Saints and Peace built, which can still be seen today, in slightly modified form, in the rue du Marais in Caen.

From then on William took more interest in the small village of Caen where he began building himself a stronghold, making it much easier to oversee his vassals in the west of the region. The people of Caen could thank Duke William for the growth of their city and its surroundings.

Normandy found peace and prosperity for a while. It is thought that, from that day onward, the Duchy took on the dimensions of a modern, powerful state, a dimension which France only achieved much later. Agriculture, craftsmanship and commerce developed, abbeys were founded. The province became prosperous. Nineteen years after this battle of Val ès dunes, the Duke would have no difficulty in financing the expedition which, from his success at Hastings, would make him King of England.

Sources

William of Poitiers and William of Jumièges, contempories of the period, have both written of the events of the rebellion by the barons of western Normandy and Gui of burgundy, along with the battle of Val ès dunes, but briefly and too succinctly for our purposes. Later, at the beginning of the 12th century, William of Malmesbury and Ordéric Vital were hardly more forthcoming. The oldest text which describes the battle in the most detail is that of Wace, written over a hundred years later in the second half of the 12th century. (Some historians believe, probably wrongly, that his first name was Robert.) It is an epic poem in 8 syllable lines called '*Le Roman de Rou*' (Rollo, first Duke of Normandy in 911) which was commissioned by Henri Plantagenêt the 2nd, a fourth-generation direct descendent of William.

Wace, who came from Jersey, was more of a poet than a historian. However, as a cleric at Saint-Étienne and later canon at Bayeux Cathedral, he was familiar with all the background sites. He wrote his work with the help of many existing documents and research into the local oral traditions.

Some years later Benoît de Sainte-Maure also wrote of the battle in his *Chronique des ducs de Normandie*, taking much of his inspiration from Wace's work but in a simpler style. Since then many authors have written on the subject. Each has brought their own contribution, their own interpretation, correcting the errors of the 12th century writers - and sometimes introducing new ones.

The most complete studies of the battle would appear to have been written and published by the Abbot Le Cointe, the parish priest of Cintheaux and of Cormelles (*Conspiration des barons normands contre Guillaume le Bâtard, duc de Normandie et la bataille du Val-ès-dunes en 1047* – Pub. E. Le Gost-Clérisse –1868) and by Michel de Boüard (*Guillaume le Conquérant* – Pub. PUF –1958). René Lepelley (*Guillaume le duc, Guillaume le roi, extraits du Roman de Rou* de Wace – Pub. Centre d'Études Normandes – 1987; Annales de Normandie may 1987) also contributed much to the study of this event.

In writing this account we stayed as faithful as possible to the ancient texts, those which are the most detailed and closest to the actual events: *Le Roman de Rou et des Ducs de Normandie* by Wace published by Frédéric Pluquet in 1877; Extracts from *le Roman de Rou by Wace,* Norman poet of the 12th century *Guillaume le duc Guillaume, le roi,* published by René Lepelley in 1987 and *Chronique des ducs de Normandie* by Benoît of Sainte-Maure, english-Norman poet of the 12th century, published by Francisque Michel in 1844. Concerning later interpretations we endeavored to be as pragmatic as possible, making the most of the knowledge of place names and of military arts of the period which was so generously shared with us by Thierry Wavelet, a master at arms, member of the Academy of Arms and former chairman of the Association of Friends of Normandy Museum.

Works of Reference

William of Jumièges (XIth century).

William of Poitiers (XIth century), *Gesta Guillelmi.*

William of Malesbury, *De Gestis Regum Anglorum*, Volume III.

Wace (XIIth century), *Roman de Rou et des Ducs de Normandie*, verse 8896 to 9336.

Benoît of Sainte-Maure (XIIth century), *Chronique des Ducs de Normandie*, verse 33160 to 33190 and *Vie de Guillaume le Conquérant* (translation by Paul Fichet, Heimdal 1976).

Ordéric Vital, Volumes I et VII.

Arcisse de Caumont, *Statistique Monumentale du Calvados*, Volume I, 1846.

Abbé Le Cointe, *Conspiration des Barons Normands contre Guillaume-Le-Bâtard Duc de Normandie et Bataille du Val-des-Dunes en 1047*, 1868.

Liliane and Fred Funcken, *Le costume, l'armure et les armes au temps de la chevalerie*, Volume I, *Du huitième au quinzième siècle*, pub. Casterman, 1977.

Michel Planchon, *Quand la Normandie était aux Vikings*, pub. Fayard, 1980.

Gilles Henry, *Guillaume le Conquérant*, pub. Charles Corlet, 1983.

Michel de Boüard, *Guillaume le Conquérant*, pub. Fayard, 1984.

René Lepelley, *Guillaume le duc Guillaume le roi*, Centre d'Études Normandes, 1987.

François Neveux, *La Normandie des ducs aux rois* 10th - 12th centuries, pub. Ouest-France Université, 1998.

Philippe Maurice, Guillaume le conquérant, pub. Flamarion, 2002.

Pierre Bouet, *Guillaume le Conquérant et les Normands au XIXe siècle*, pub. Charles Corlet, 2003.

Paul Zumthor, *Guillaume le Conquérant*, pub. Tallandier, 2003.

Philippe Contamine, *La guerre au Moyen Âge*, pub. PUF, 2003.

David Bates, *William the Conqueror* (in english), Tempus Publishing, 2004.

Pierre Bouet et François Neveux, *Les villes au Moyen Âge*, 2006.

Stéphane Laîné, *La Fuite de Valognes : comparaison des différentes versions en langue vernaculaire* (in *Guillaume le Conquérant face aux défis*, texts collected by Huguette Legros), pub. Paradigme, 2008.

Pierre Bouet, *Hastings*, pub.Tallandier, 2010.

Antony Holden, *Le Roman de Rou*, 3 volumes,Wace, pub. Holden, 2011.

François Neveux, *Guillaume le Conquérant*, pub. Ouest-France, 2013.

Christopher Gravett, Christa Hook, David Nicolle and Karen Watts, *Norman knight 950 – 1204 AD. Weapons, armour, tactics. Warior series 1*, pub. Osprey military, réimp. 1998.

It is well known that history is not an exact science. Most particularly in the present case we have drawn from sources that owe more to epic narratives than to historic chronicles. Like so many studies this paper is the result of a pooling of knowledge which may readily be supplemented and even challenged by new theories and ideas.

THANKS

We wish to thank most sincerely Professor Lucien Musset, Professor René Lepelley, Pierre Bouet, Honourary Maître de Conférence at Caen University specializing in Latin authors of the 11th and 12th centuries, Christophe Maneuvrier, Maître de Conférence in Mediaeval history at Caen University, Jean Desloges from the archeological department of the Regional Department of Cultural Affairs for Basse-Normandie and Thierry Wavelet, master of arms, who all helped, each in their own field, in the creation of the first edition of this work in 2003.

We would also like to thank Stéphane Laîné, Dr of the Science of Language, Normandy University, Unicaen, CRISCO (EA4255), who lectures at Caen University and Rennes 2 University. He kindly made several contributions to this second edition (2016), with great pertinence.

We were fortunate enough to be able to collaborate with Fabien Drugeon, script-writer, film-maker and director of photography on the film *Guillaume, la jeunesse du Conquérant* © Les films du Cartel. He allowed us to use stills from that film to illustrate this booklet. We thank him warmly, along with Jean-Damien Détouillon (Guillaume in 1047), Bruno Bayeux (King Henri), Lucien Duchemin (White rider), Tiesay Deshayes (William as a child) and Eric Rulliat (Ranulf).

Produced by Cartel films, *William, the youth of the Conqueror* is a feature film telling the story of Duke William's youth. With limited means Fabien Drugeon has created a vast historical panorama which succeeds in conveying all the richness of the period. This artistic work does not always stick to the bare facts as we know them but Fabien Drugeon creates an authenticity of time and place, of costume and battle which conjure up the real spirit of the past.

(Photo opposite : During the Mediaeval Val ès dunes Festival at Argences in 2013, Fabien Drugeon is taking photos for his film.)

Fabien Drugeon.
© Photo Jean-Paul Hauguel

We also thank Emmanuel Cerisier to allow us to reproduce the portrait of William (p. 3) from the book *Château de Guillaume le Conquérant Falaise* by OREP publishing.
Finally we would like to pay tribute to Christian Lechevalier, ex-chairman of the Tourism Office, and to Xavier Pichon, chairman of the Communauté de Communes of Val ès dunes who were the instigators of this history of the battle.

DISCOVERING THE SITE OF THE BATTLE

To help visitors discover the battle site, the community of villages of Val ès dunes has installed information panels in eight different places.

A leaflet is available at the tourist Office.

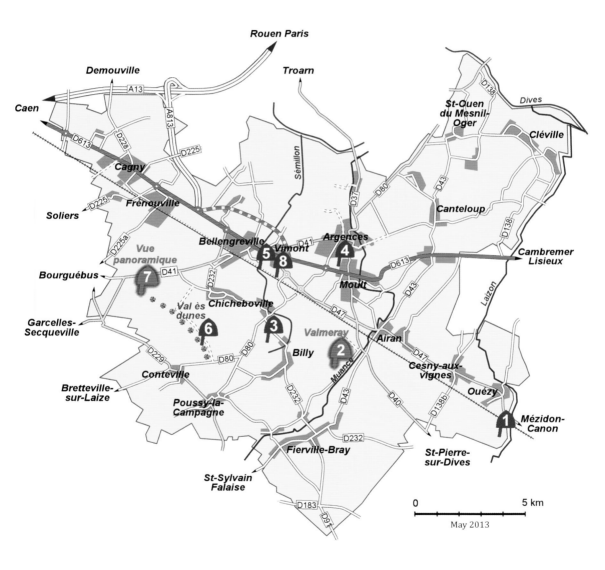

Where Henri the 1st made camp

Les Forges d'Ouézy (along the river Laizon, at the entrance of Canon)
N 49° 04' 32,48" – W 0° 05' 51,75"

 The army of Henri 1st gets into battle formation and the King attends Mass

Airan - Valmeray
N 49° 05' 45,43" – W 0° 09' 47,18"

 Gathering of the armies of William, Henri and the peasants

Chicheboville - Béneauville
N 49° 06' 13 46" – W 0° 11' 58,20"

 Site of William's encampment before the battle.

Argences
N 49° 07' 36,05" – W 0° 09 52,70"

 Bérenger Ford, on the William's route

Vimont - Church
N 49° 07' 22,11" – W 0° 12' 01,98"

 The battlefield

3rd wind turbine north of RD 80
N 49° 05' 55,35" – W 0° 13' 43.78"

 Commemorative plaque and panoramic view

Bellengreville RD 41
N 49° 06' 58,68" – W 0° 14' 51,54"

 Commemorative plaque of 1841

Vimont RD 613 Est
N 49° 07' 16,32" – W 0° 11' 36,49"

Permanent information boards.

At point n°8 is the commemorative plaque erected by Arcisse de Caumont in 1841, on the side of the D 613 road, at the eastern end of Vimont. In those days, it was the closest site to the battlefield accessible by a good road. We also know that the historian made a mistake in the location of the Bérenger Ford.

The Val ès dunes battle is one among twelve sites in "The fabulous épic of William the Conqueror" created by the tourist board of the department of Calvados. The site of the battle is indicated by two orange information panels located at points 7 and 8.

Another commemorative plaque was erected by Léonard Gille (general counselor) in 1949. It is located on the D 41 road, 750 metres before the crossroad with the D 89 road. On this occasion, a large medieval festival was organized in the main town of the district, Bourguébus. Station n° 7 was constructed in 2012 with an orientation table and an information panel.

Design by Fanny
Lechevalier-Lafon.

OREP Éditions, Zone tertiaire de Nonant, 14400 BAYEUX
Tel: 02 31 51 81 31 – **Fax:** 02 31 51 81 32
info@orepeditions.com – www.orepeditions.com

Éditor: Grégory PIQUE – **Conception design:** Éditions OREP
Graphics and layout: Sophie YOUF
Editorial coordination: Kévin DECROUY
Translation: Sara van Beers and Henri Roussel

ISBN: 978-2-8151-0294-0
Copyright OREP 2016 – Legal Deposit: 3rd quarter 2016